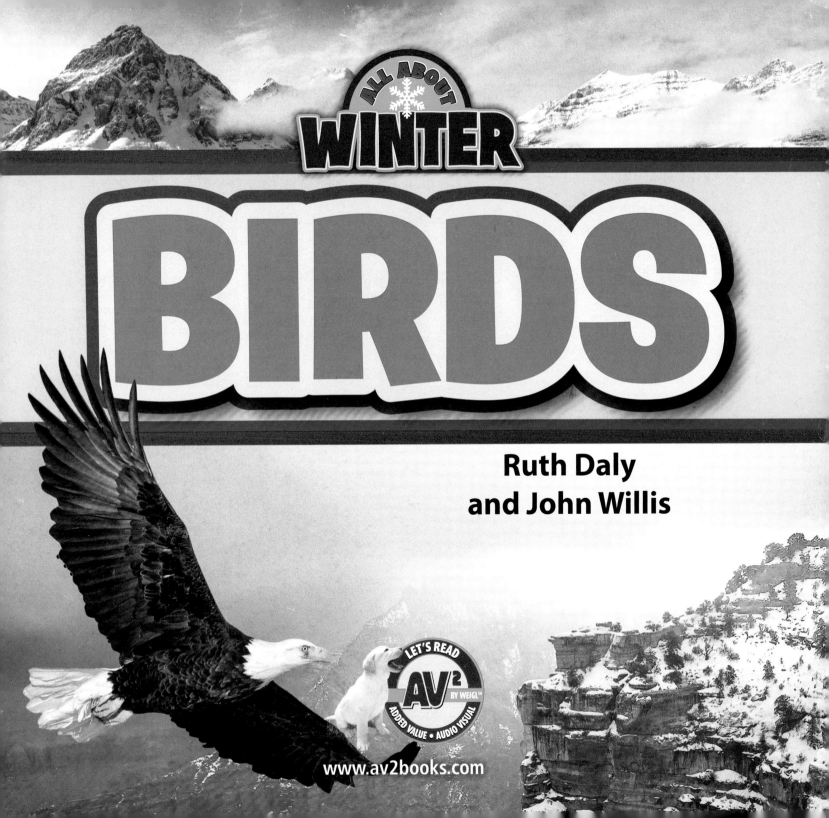

ALL ABOUT WINTER

BIRDS

**Ruth Daly
and John Willis**

LET'S READ
AV²
BY WEIGL™
ADDED VALUE • AUDIO VISUAL

Go to **www.av2books.com**,
and enter this book's
unique code.

BOOK CODE

AVS49395

AV² by Weigl brings you media
enhanced books that support
active learning.

AV² provides enriched content that supplements and complements this book. Weigl's AV² books strive to create inspired learning and engage young minds in a total learning experience.

Your AV² Media Enhanced books come alive with...

Audio
Listen to sections of
the book read aloud.

Video
Watch informative
video clips.

Embedded Weblinks
Gain additional information
for research.

Try This!
Complete activities and
hands-on experiments.

Key Words
Study vocabulary, and
complete a matching
word activity.

Quizzes
Test your knowledge.

Slide Show
View images and
captions, and prepare
a presentation.

... and much, much more!

Published by AV² by Weigl
350 5th Avenue, 59th Floor   New York, NY 10118
Website: www.av2books.com

Library of Congress Cataloging-in-Publication Data
Names: Daly, Ruth, 1962- author. I Willis, John, 1989- author.
Title: Birds. All about winter / Ruth Daly and John Willis.
Other titles: All about winter
Description: Published by. I New York : AV2 by Weigl, [2019] I Audience: K to grade 3. I Includes index.
Identifiers: LCCN 2018053463 (print) I LCCN 2018059510 (ebook) I ISBN 9781489697073 (Multi User ebook) I
ISBN 9781489697080 (Single User ebook) I ISBN 9781489697059 (hardcover : alk. paper) I ISBN 9781489697066 (softcover : alk. paper)
Classification: LCC QL698.3 (ebook) I LCC QL698.3 .D365 2019 (print) I DDC 598--dc23
LC record available at https://lccn.loc.gov/2018053463

Printed in the United States of America in Brainerd, Minnesota
1 2 3 4 5 6 7 8 9 0 22 21 20 19 18

122018
102918

Project Coordinator: John Willis   Designer: Ana María Vidal

Every reasonable effort has been made to trace ownership and to obtain permission to reprint copyright material.
The publishers would be pleased to have any errors or omissions brought to their attention so that they may be corrected in subsequent printings.
Weigl acknowledges Alamy, iStock,and Shutterstock as the primary image suppliers for this title.

BIRDS

In this book, you will learn about

what they are

what they do

how they change

and much more!

Finding Food

It is winter. The days are short. It is cold outside. There is not much food.

🌎 In Utqiaġvik, Alaska, the Sun does not rise for 67 days each winter.

5

6

Plants do not grow.
Birds are hungry.
They work hard to find
food and water.

Birds look for food together.
They find berries and
seeds to eat.

8

A blue jay may hide about 3,000 acorns each year to save for winter.

9

10

Birds have special feathers called down. These are soft and fluffy. Down keeps birds warm.

Winter nights are cold.
Birds roost close together.
They roost in evergreens
and inside bushes.

13

14

People can put up bird boxes.
Birds shelter here from the wind.

As many as 12 birds may share a bird box to keep warm.

People also hang bird
feeders from trees.
They fill them with seeds.

16

18

Birds eat from bird feeders. People often watch them eating in their backyards.

Birds do not sing as often in winter. It is too much work. They wait for spring to start.

20

Some birds sing in winter to **chase away** other birds.

21

Recycled Bird Feeder

Make a milk carton bird feeder!

Supplies:

- 1 milk carton
- bird seed
- scissors
- non-toxic paint
- string
- wooden spoon

Instructions:

1. Wash and dry the milk carton.

2. Cut a hole in two opposite sides of the carton, about half way down. Decorate it with paint.

3. Make small holes about one inch below the large holes. Push a wooden spoon through the holes. Birds can land on the spoon to eat the seeds.

4. Add bird seed to fill the carton up to the large holes.

5. Thread string through the top of the carton and hang it from a tree.

KEY WORDS

Research has shown that as much as 65 percent of all written material published in English is made up of 300 words. These 300 words cannot be taught using pictures or learned by sounding them out. They must be recognized by sight. This book contains 57 common sight words to help young readers improve their reading fluency and comprehension. This book also teaches young readers several important content words, such as proper nouns. These words are paired with pictures to aid in learning and improve understanding.

Page	Sight Words First Appearance
4	are, days, food, is, it, much, not, the, there
5	does, each, for, in, sets
7	and, do, find, grow, hard, plants, they, to, water, work
8	eat, look, together
9	a, about, may, year
11	down, have, keeps, these
12	close, nights
15	as, can, from, here, many, people, put, up
16	also, them, trees, with
19	often, their, watch
20	start, too
21	away, other, some

Page	Content Words First Appearance
4	winter
5	Sun, Utqiaġvik, Alaska
7	birds
8	berries, seeds
9	acorns, blue jay
11	feathers
12	bushes, evergreens
15	bird boxes, wind
16	bird feeders
20	spring

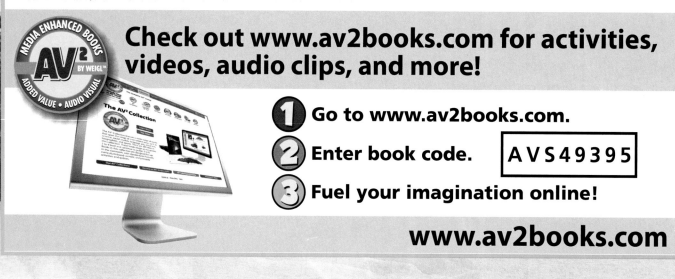